Winter Signs
in
the Snow

by
Gerald Cox

Calligraphy by
Kitty Weaver

Michael Kesend Publishing, Ltd.
New York

Dedicated to
DYKE WILLIAMS
and his
country ways

Copyright 1975 © Gerald Cox
Revised Edition 1984

Fifth Printing—1988

"Wintersigns" illustrates selected natural tracks and features of snowy woods, lakes, meadows and mountains in the northern United States and southern Canada.

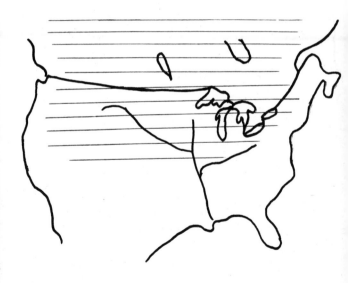

Contents

Wintersigns

The tracks follow the edge of the lake, wandering yet purposeful. Who passed this way? These "wintersigns" in the snow ghost over a fallen log, poke at several places into a brush pile, circle the muskrat house in the pond.

The trackmaker - a Red Fox - must have dug these holes in the snow looking for mice - his favorite food. His tracks go on, overlapping the prints of a Cottontail, and both sets continue into the quiet of the woods.

"Wintersigns" can be a magnet, drawing us along paths in the snow. They often tell an exciting story. They are visible proof that the "dead of winter" is really full of life.

Reading the winter landscape is easy though sometimes it calls for a bit of detective work. The elements can play tricks — the sun can greatly enlarge a tiny print and can distort or completely fill in the biggest print.

Sometimes our "summer" assumptions about animals and their habitats are just plain wrong in the reality of winter. Several animals have adapted so they live above, on or under the snow, depending upon how they are built or choose to live.

The moose and deer have "stilt" legs holding their bodies above the snow. The Snowshoe Rabbit has - you guessed it - "snowshoe"- like feet for traveling on the surface of the snow. The mouse, however, tunnels under the snow where it can stay away from the extreme cold and its many enemies.

Adaptation For Life in Deep Snow

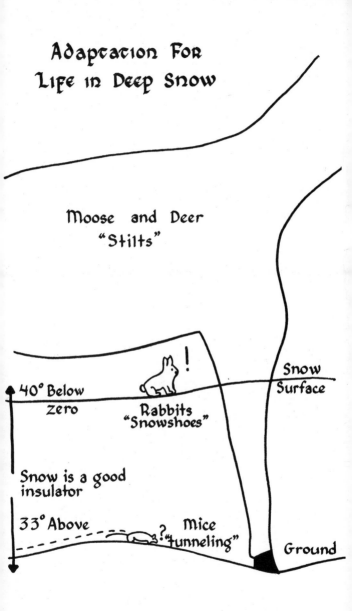

Moose and Deer
"Stilts"

Snow Surface

40° Below Zero

Rabbits "Snowshoes"

Snow is a good insulator

33° Above

Mice "tunneling"

Ground

Rabbits

←—8"-30"—→|←—6"-12"—→|

←|3"|←

Cottontail Tracks

During winters of deep
snow, rabbits often eat
bark which sometimes
kills saplings.

←—5"-20"—→

←—10"-12"—→

Snowshoe
Rabbit tracks
have fuzzy edges
caused by big hairy feet.
The rabbit is a large, white,
northern woodland dweller. Like
the Snowshoe, the Cottontail is also
a woodland dweller and their tracks
become packed highways.

"Rabbit forms" are pockets in snow melted by body heat when a rabbit takes shelter.

Rabbit scat about ½ actual size

Twigs eaten by rabbits are cut at angles.

Jack Rabbits are large, speedy, open area dwellers with very large ears.

Fox-Coyote

|← 8"-10" →|

When walking, fox and coyote tracks are commonly found in a straight line. The coyote track will be larger than Red or Gray Fox tracks.

Following a trail can lead to a kill marked by feathers, fur, blood and bones.

Look for dens in hollow logs, rock piles or in enlarged woodchuck dens on well drained hill sides.

The coyote tends to be more of an open area dweller than the fox and is usually nocturnal.

|←—1½"-2"—→|

The Red and Gray Fox and coyote have tracks about the same size.

Remember, sun and wind can change the details.

The scat are about 2 inches long; the contents may be mouse hair and bones or rabbit fur and bones.

Wolf

Wolf droppings usually have much hair in them and are often deposited in plain sight.

Tracks are commonly found in open areas and on lakes but packs of three or more usually seek shelter in denser vegetation.

The wolf is found in only a few areas with the greatest numbers in northeastern Minnesota and Canada.

Dog

Tracks of the domestic dog cannot be generalized because of the great size variation. Tracks of the canine family (dog, fox, wolf) usually show a claw mark because the claws are not retractable as they are in the cat family.

The observer must judge largely on the size of the tracks and the nearness to human habitation. Tame dog droppings usually would not have hair in them.

Beaver

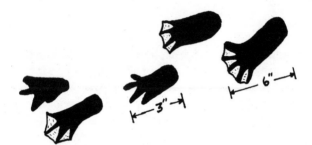

Beaver tracks are about 3-5 inches apart but are not plain because the drag of the wide tail brushes them out. These tracks are seldom seen in the winter since the beavers tend to stay in their lodges under the ice.

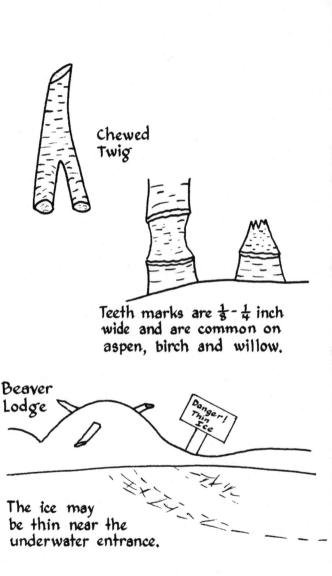

Chewed
Twig

Teeth marks are $\frac{1}{8} - \frac{1}{4}$ inch
wide and are common on
aspen, birch and willow.

Beaver
Lodge

Danger!
Thin
Ice

The ice may
be thin near the
underwater entrance.

Other Snow and Ice Danger Spots

DANGER!

Ice is thinner where streams leave or enter bodies of water and where there are under water springs.

Use caution
when gurgling
water can be heard
under ice or snow. The
moving water can mean
thin ice or no ice at all.

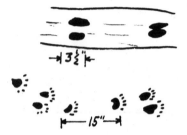

Otter tracks are some-
what indistinct, set in a
trough of snow made
by passage of the
otter's body.

Otter slides are common
where they "frolic" in the
snow & down embankments.

Air holes are found in the ice and may be
used by otter, mink or beaver. They spend
much time under the ice where they
catch fish, crayfish and other prey.

Marten and Fisher

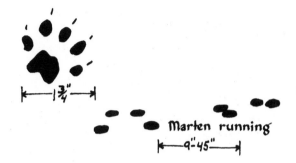

|← 1¾" →|

Marten running

|← 9"-45" →|

Marten

These relatively rare animals are found in the northern pine forests. Marten tracks can easily be confused with mink.

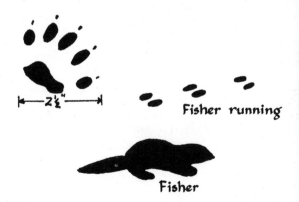

|← 2½" →|

Fisher running

Fisher

Mink

→|1½"|←

|←—12"-20"—→|

When walking, the rear print usually does not show because the mink commonly step in their own tracks. When running, all four tracks may show.

Mink are commonly found along stream edges, lakes and drainage ditches.

|←3"-4"→|

Mink droppings vary in texture and color depending on diet. Look for bones and feathers.

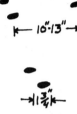

← 10"-13" →

→|1¾"|←

Weasel

(called Ermine in winter white)

Weasels are small with white bodies 6-10 inches long. Their trails are often erratic with tunnels where the trail disappears and reappears. The rear track often falls into the front track so they appear as twins. Weasel tracks can be found near barns, rocks, logs or any other safe area. They tend to store food for future use so one may find caches of bodies of mice or other small animals.

Weasel droppings are similar to mink droppings only smaller.

Cats

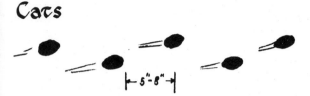

|← 5"-8" →|

Domestic Cat

There are usually no claw marks because cats have retractable claws. Single tracks are about 1-1½ inches in size. The droppings are similar to fox but the cat usually covers it by scratching snow or debris over it.

|← 2" →|

|← 10" →|

Bobcat & Lynx

|← 4"-6" →|

|← 12" →|

Pad prints are not distinct because of the furry paws. This is especially true in soft snow.

Mountain Lion!

|← 3"–3½" →|

Really? There have been
occasional reports of large
cat sightings in the north-
east corner of Minnesota.
Tracks are about 22 inches
apart. Look for a light
colored large cat with a
long tail.

Skunk

Skunks generally sleep during most of the winter but on a warm winter night they may wander out.

Their tracks show a trail which seems to wind about aimlessly.

Skunks are not as quick to spray their protective weapon as many think. They can be observed at a reasonable distance in reasonable safety.

Raccoon

Raccoons are not true hibernators so they will be out during the winter.

In the northern states they mate in January and February.

They den up in hollow trees and will leave at night to look for food.

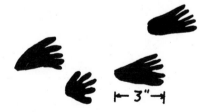

|— 3" —|

Squirrels

Gray or "Fox" Squirrel tracks in the snow between trees. Fox Squirrel tracks are larger with more distinct toe tracks. <u>Chipmunks</u> are sleeping in the winter.

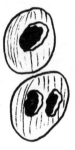

Gray and Fox Squirrels usually eat one hole on each side of a walnut.

Flying Squirrels usually eat four holes in walnuts, two on each side.

A Flying Squirrel's tracks may appear out of nowhere as it glides to a landing. Its skin flaps leave a distinct mark when landing.

During the day it may nest in old bird nests, hollow trees or have its own leaf nest in a tree crotch. They are usually about only at night and thus are hard to spot.

Red Squirrels are a more northern animal. They tend to scold any intruder and leave piles of pine cone remains where they have eaten out the pine cones. The tracks are similar to the Gray Squirrel only smaller.

Muskrat

There is a distinct narrow tail drag mark, and the front print usually lands inside of the rear print. These tracks are rarely seen in winter.

Muskrat houses are about three feet in diameter and are made of cattails and other marsh plants.

The ice may be thin
near the house.

Muskrat dropping shown
about actual size, but is
rarely seen during the
winter.

Mice

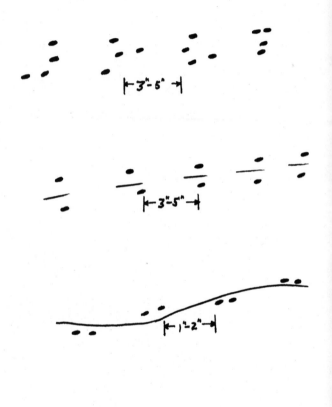

Mice commonly tunnel under the snow but the tracks may appear briefly on the surface when the mouse tunnels out and back into the snow

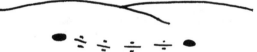

While above the snow, mice are prey for hawks, owls and other predators.

Mouse tracks may also be found on snow covered logs and branches, for some mice live in old bird nests.

Shrew tracks and tunnels are similar but smaller.

Porcupine

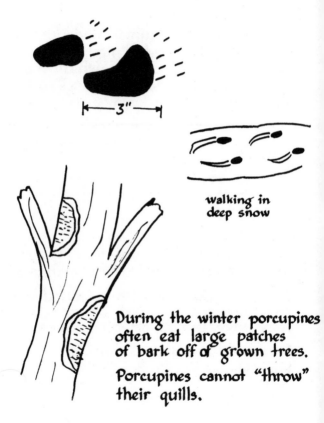

|← 3" →|

walking in
deep snow

During the winter porcupines
often eat large patches
of bark off of grown trees.

Porcupines cannot "throw"
their quills.

Bear

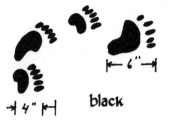

|← 6" →|

|→ 4" ←|

black

The possibilities of seeing a bear in the winter are slim. Because they are not true hibernators they may come out for a very short time.

Should you find a sleeping bear under a windfall or hollow don't disturb it.

grizzly

|← 12" →|

|← 6" →|

Antelope

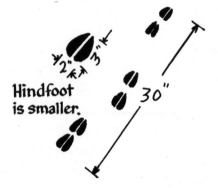

Hindfoot is smaller.

2" 3" 30"

Tracks are easily confused with Mule Deer which are usually in the same range. This is a wide open space animal.

Mountain Sheep

Tracks are not as
pointed as deer;
have straighter sides.

When trying to identify
similar split-hoofed tracks
one must consider if the
suspected track maker would
be in that particular environment.
The Big Horn Sheep would often
be around mountain ledges.

Elk

Tracks are larger and
rounder than deer.
Can be confused with
young cattle.

Look for the
gnawed aspen
trees in high elk
populated areas.

Mountain Goat

Tracks similar to Big Horn
but toes spread outward.

→ 3½" ←

The goat tends to be on
the higher cliffs and crags.

Deer

|← 3½" →| →|15"-20"|←

Drag marks from hooves are common when walking in snow.

When deer move in very deep snow they may leave a trough with depressions in it where they have to lunge forward to make any headway.

Deer dropping about actual size.

Moose

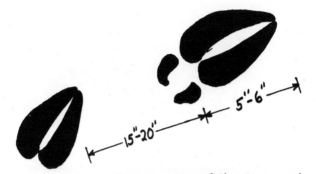

|← 15"-20" →| |← 5"-6" →|

Drag marks of the legs and body may block out the print. Look for beds where the moose (and deer) sleep, packing down the snow, showing smooth curves of the body. Broken willows are a sign of feeding.

Dropping of common size.

Birds

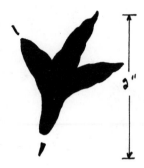

2"

Grouse often spend time
buried under snow and may
explode out leaving a ragged
hole with wing tip marks
on either side.

**Grouse
dropping**

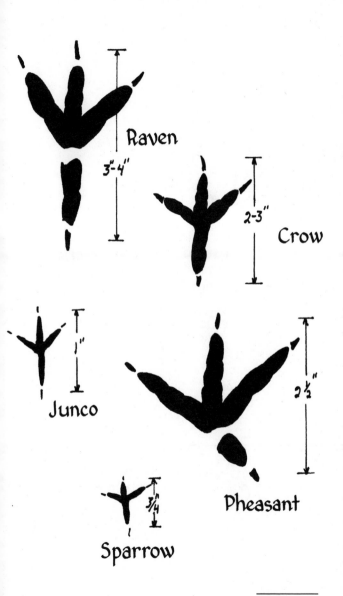

Raven

3"-4"

Crow

2-3"

Junco

1"

Pheasant

2½"

Sparrow

¾"

Birds

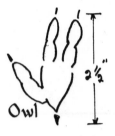

Owl

2½"

Barred Owl and Great
Horned Owl tracks are
about the same size.

2"

Owl pellets are "belched" up and spit out
and are commonly found under perching
trees. The pellet contains undigestable bone
and hair —   usually of mice.

The end of the trail for
a mouse is shown by a
depression & wing marks.

Canada
Goose

Mallard

Ducks and geese may linger after winter freeze up if patches of open water remain.

Woodpeckers will attack a tree, Cedar commonly, making "machine gun-like" holes in the bark as they go after insects.

Common Trees

Winter tree identification is not as difficult as one might think.

There are some characteristics which allow for general grouping.

For example:

Maple, Ash, Dogwood and Buckeye trees all have opposite branching. Taking the first letter of each tree plus the buck from buckeye spells MAD-BUCK.

Applying that to the trees, one can more easily identify the winter trees.

Maple

general shape

opposite twig

branches

winged seeds

buds smooth,
purplish-brown

Ash

opposite

MAD-BUCK

general shape

seed shaped like
blade of canoe
paddle

Buds also opposite
if twigs are
opposite

brown - black

Dogwood

general shape

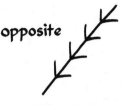

opposite

MAD-BUCK

Enlarged flower buds.
Flowering dogwood.

Twigs on the
branches all
seem to point
upward.

There are some
exceptions to the
alternate branching
in dogwoods.

Buckeye

general shape

opposite branching

MAD-BUCK

brown buds

Prickly cover over the buckeye which is about 1-2 inches in diameter.

Horse chestnut is very similar. Look for black bud.

Birch

general shape

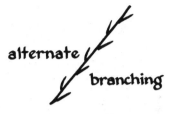

alternate branching

Bark is chalky white with curls hanging. Horizontal black marks on bark. Color will vary with species.

Twigs smooth, hairy. Buds pointed. Look for cone-like catkins.

Aspen

alternate

branching
on twigs

general shape

The aspen is often
mistaken for birch.
Aspen bark is smooth
and greenish to gray.
It is not curly like
birch. Old aspen bark
is usually dark and
furrowed.

In mountains
whole groves
of aspen may
be bent from the
movement of the
snow
pack.

Aspen buds
look varnished—
brown to black.

Evergreen Needles

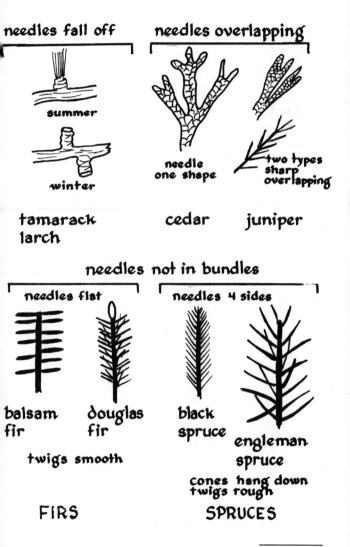

needles fall off

summer

winter

tamarack
larch

needles overlapping

needle
one shape

two types
sharp
overlapping

cedar   juniper

needles not in bundles

needles flat

balsam   douglas
fir   fir

twigs smooth

FIRS

needles 4 sides

black
spruce

engleman
spruce

cones hang down
twigs rough

SPRUCES

Cedar

The northern white cedar
is mostly a Great Lakes,
Southern Canada, Appalachian
species. It grows to about
50 feet.

The needles are
overlapping like
shingles giving
the branch a soft,
flat spray appear-
ance; common along
lake shores.

Cones are $\frac{1}{2}$
inch long -
brown.

Look for the deer browse line.
The bottom branches are all
trimmed to the same level -
as high as a deer can reach.

Junipers

Junipers have two kinds of needles; sharp awl-like needles and overlapping scales like cedar.

They also have a bluish berry-like cone about ¼ inch in diameter. If you bite into the berry it tastes like gin. It used to be used in flavoring gin.

There are several species of junipers. Some are trees — some are small. They grow in the flat lands and high mountain areas.

Tamarack (Larch)

This is not a true evergreen because the needles drop off each fall. Many people wonder what killed all those pines in the swamp. Usually they are asking about live tamarack.

The Indians used the roots for sewing their canoes. The cones are less than an inch.

The western larch is similar except much larger, up to 200 feet. The needles are longer, 1-1½ inch, the cones are 1-1½ inch and tend to be upright on the branches.

Balsam Fir

This tree's range is along the Great Lake states and Southern Canada.

The needles are flat and arranged as though parted with a comb.

The cones are 2-3 inches long and stand upright on a branch like a candle.

Deer, moose and porcupine eat the twigs. Grouse eat the seeds.

The smooth bark has large resinous blisters. Indians used the resin for their canoes and the resin was sold as gum before modern chewing gum.

Douglas Fir

Soft, flat needles
on drooping
twigs. There are
long pointed
brown buds at the
tips of the twigs.

Look for 3-4 inch
cones with bracts
extending from under
the scales. The bracts
resemble the tail and
back feet of mice.

This is a western tree which
can become very tall.

Black/White Spruce

Both trees grow in the same geographic area. They can be difficult to tell apart. The black grows in boggy areas, the white in drier areas.

black   white

Black needles are $\frac{1}{4}$ - $\frac{1}{2}$ inch long, white $\frac{1}{2}$ - $\frac{3}{4}$ inch long. New twigs of black spruce are hairy; white not hairy. You will need a magnifying glass to see it.

The cones of the black are $\frac{1}{2}$ - 1 inch and stay on the tree for years. Cones of the white are 1-2 inches – falling off when ripe.

Colorado Blue Spruce

This is a very attractive tree
found in the Rocky Mountains.
In most other areas it is planted.

The needles are 4 sided as are
all spruce, and are a dull blue-geen.
The 1- 1½ inch needles are very
prickly.

Look for it along streams, mixed
with other species and on north-
facing, hence shaded, more
moist slopes.

Engleman Spruce

The tree has shorter needles,
about ½ - 1 inch, than blue spruce.
Look for the typical downward
hanging cone.

The needles have a strong, and to
some, disagreeable odor when
crushed.

This tree can be 100-150 feet
tall and 1-3 feet in diameter.
Look for this tree in the Rockies
at an elevation of 9,000 - 11,500
feet. That is the subalpine
zone with heavy snowfall, much
vegetation.

Evergreen Needles

needles in bunches

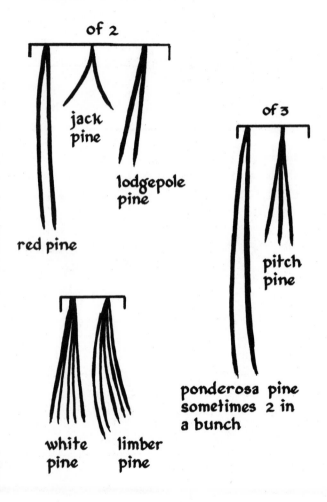

of 2

jack
pine

lodgepole
pine

red pine

of 3

pitch
pine

ponderosa pine
sometimes 2 in
a bunch

white
pine

limber
pine

Jack Pine

This is sometimes called the fire pine because it is often the first pine to grow after a fire.

There are two needles - ¾ - 1½ inches long which spread apart.

The cone is 1-2 inches long, closed very tightly, growing very hard to the branch and will remain on the tree for years.

Limber Pine

The needles are 5-10 in a bunch and curved. White pine are straight and softer.

In sheltered areas it may grow from 25-50 feet tall.

It is also a timberline tree growing at an elevation of 10,000 -11,500 feet.

In those exposed conditions it may become a stunted, gnarled tree 1-2 feet tall with branches on one side.

prevailing wind

Lodgepole Pine

Look for 2 needles per bunch with the needles often twisted. The needles are 1-3 inches long.

The cones are one sided and egg-shaped.

Young stands of lodgepole grow close together making slender straight trunks which the Indians used for lodgepoles.

It grows on the lower slopes of the Rocky Mountains.

Pitch Pine

This 50 foot tree generally
follows the Appalachian
Mountains into Southeast
Ontario.

The cones are 2-3 inches long
and have sharp spines.

The needles are 3 in a bunch,
about 3 inches long.

Pitch flows when the bark is
broken. The knots are very
pitchy and were used as torches
by the pioneers.

Ponderosa Pine

The needles are three to a bunch, sometimes two, and they are very long, 5-7 inches long.

This is a big tree of 150 feet and more with a diameter of 3-4 feet. It is found in the lower elevations of the Rocky Mountains around 6,000 - 9,000 feet.

The cones are 3-6 inches long with sharp spines.

The bark is reddish-orange and looks like a jigsaw puzzle.

Red Pine or Norway Pine

The needles are in twos;
4-5 inches long and are brittle.

Look for a cone about
two inches long.

The bark is reddish
and the branches
stick out horizontally
from the trunk.

The tree looks
rugged and coarse.

White Pine

The needles
are 5 to a
bunch and are
3-5 inches long.

The branches project
upward from the
trunk as in a smile.

Look for 4-5 inch slender
cones in the snow because
the cones fall off in the
winter.

The tree appears to have
a soft, delicate texture.

Inanimate Wonders

Leaf

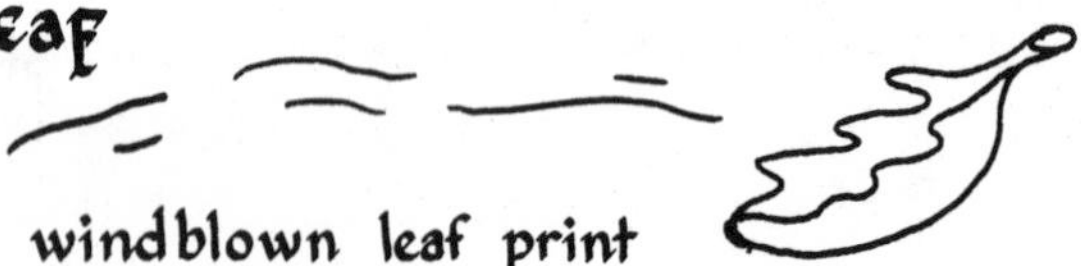

A windblown leaf print
often resembles a mouse track.

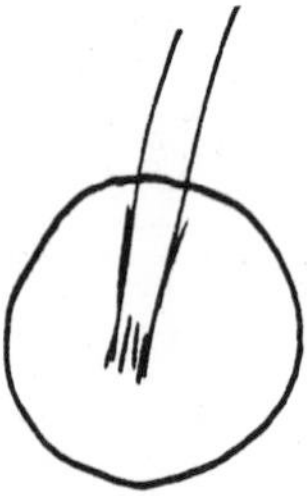

Circles

Nearly perfect circles in
the snow are caused by
grass stems which the
wind whips around.

Cavities Around Trees

These holes are caused by wind currents and heat from the sun attracted by the dark colored tree bark.

In some areas, the cavities can be large enough for an adult to fall into.

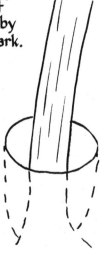

Broken Brush

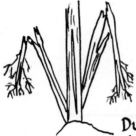

During mating season deer often spar with bushes and also rub their newly formed antlers on brush to remove the drying velvet.

Tree Tracks

Clumps of snow often
fall from tree branches
causing holes in the snow
which may resemble
animal tracks.

Rock and Leaf Tables

A stone or leaf on the
snow can slow the
melting of snow under-
neath and cause the
object to become
supported on a pillar.

Sounds

A beauty of winter is often the lack of sound. Some, however, are soft and subtle; others occur with startling suddenness.

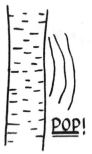

POP!

As the temperature drops during the cold of a winter night or early morning, the trees may resound... <u>LOUDLY</u>.

During the witching hours of the brightest Northern Lights some have said "I heard them whisper."

Trees may
"groan" as they
are rubbed one against another. The
wind may "rattle" the branches together
in their icy nakedness.

The wind will cause the snow to "hiss"
as it sculptures in free form or one
can hear a faint "murmur" as the
snow seems to speak where flowing
water runs beneath.

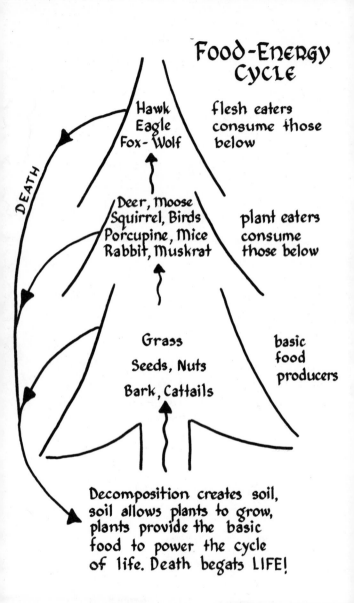

Food-Energy Cycle

Hawk
Eagle
Fox-Wolf

flesh eaters consume those below

DEATH

Deer, Moose
Squirrel, Birds
Porcupine, Mice
Rabbit, Muskrat

plant eaters consume those below

Grass

Seeds, Nuts

Bark, Cattails

basic food producers

Decomposition creates soil,
soil allows plants to grow,
plants provide the basic
food to power the cycle
of life. Death begats LIFE!

Sightings - Notes